CUPCAKES &
Cocktails

About Bonnie Marcus

Bonnie Marcus launched her stylish stationery company, the Bonnie Marcus Collection 'where fashion meets paper®', in 2002 from her dining room table, while expecting her first child. As a former wedding planner in New York City, Marcus was well known for her event planning expertise and found there was a void in the stationery market in terms of fashion-forward stylish designs. She decided to combine her passion for fashion (having worked for designer Diane Von Furstenberg) with her love of event planning and her collection took the stationery industry by storm! Bonnie's stylish designs are now available in thousands of retail stores worldwide and celebrity fans include Cindy Crawford, Christina Aguilera, Britney Spears, Eva Longoria, Marcia Cross and many others. Marcus has been recognized as a pioneer for women in business and is proud to be an established partner of the Breast Cancer Research Foundation® and Autism Speaks®. For further information about the company, please visit www.bonniemarcus.com.

CUPCAKES &
Cocktails

Fabulous cupcake and cocktail recipes for any occasion

Bonnie Marcus Collection

This edition published under license by Exclusive Editions Publishing Ltd in 2014

Exclusive Editions Publishing Ltd
Chartist House
15–17 Trim Street
Bath BA1 1HA, UK

Copyright © 2013–2014
Illustrations supplied courtesy of the © Bonnie Marcus Collection

Project managed by Annabel King
Additional text by Robin Donovan
Internal design by Lisa McCormick

ISBN 978-1-4723-2976-9

Printed in China

Notes for the Reader
A standard measure contains 25 ml.
This book uses both metric and imperial measurements. Follow the same units of measurement throughout; do not mix metric and imperial. All spoon measurements are level: teaspoons are assumed to be 5 ml, and tablespoons are assumed to be 15 ml. Unless otherwise stated, milk is assumed to be full-fat, eggs and individual vegetables are medium, and pepper is freshly ground black pepper. Unless otherwise stated, all root vegetables should be washed in plain water and peeled prior to using.

The times given are an approximate guide only. Preparation times differ according to the techniques used by different people and the cooking times may also vary from those given. Optional ingredients, variations or serving suggestions have not been included in the time calculations.

Contents

Cupcakes and Cocktails Introduction

Like whiskers on kittens and brown paper packages tied up with string, cupcakes and cocktails are two of our favourite things. Happily, we're not alone in our love of fanciful alcoholic beverages and whimsical single-serving cakes. Both have enjoyed a surge in popularity in recent years, spawning entirely new cultures of studied aficionados and devoted fans. And, let's face it, few things have more appeal. Properly made and adorned, both are a feast for the eyes and the palate.

Combining these two popular cultural phenomena can make for a uniquely modern take on the old standbys of drinks and hors d'oeuvres, wine and cheese, or crisps and beer. Think up any excuse for a party and break out the baking tins and shakers to combine these two hot trends in one colourful, delicious spread. Even if you can't drum up a good reason to celebrate, cocktails and cupcakes, all on their own, are welcome excuses for a luxuriously cosy night in. Here, you'll find recipes for both cupcakes and cocktails, as well as theme and decorating ideas to strike just the right note for any occasion.

Cupcakes are one of the world's most perfect foods – sinfully decadent, delightfully delicious and made in perfectly proportioned individual servings. And, as luck would have it, each and every one delivers the perfect ratio of icing to cake. With the endless possibilities for flavour combinations and themes, they are as much fun to bake and decorate as they are to eat. Here, you'll find cupcakes in a range of flavours, some based on cocktail recipes (and with the alcohol baked right in) and some designed simply to be the perfect match for a well-mixed drink. And as a bonus, we've included some delicious desserts recipes!

Once baked, cupcakes are a blank canvas ready to be adorned in honour of whatever you want to celebrate – an engagement, wedding, anniversary, new job, new house or even just to reward yourself for getting through another long day at work.

Cocktails, too, allow for a ton of creativity, from flavour combining to garnishing. Whether you're going for a 'fun with the girls' vibe or something more romantic, there's a cupcake and cocktail combination that will set just the right tone.

Whatever the occasion – whether you're entertaining a crowd or simply craving a sweet treat on a quiet night in – get creative, mixing and matching flavours and decorations.

The Perfect Combination

Pairing decadent cupcakes and fancy cocktails is an amazing way to set the mood, whether for a quiet night in, a casual gathering of close friends or even a huge bash.

For a casual night in, there is nothing better than a cupcake and cocktail. They offer an easy, single serving of luxury that cannot be beaten. Perfectly baked cupcakes, swirls of icing, encased in a pretty paper wrapper, all make for cupcakes that look as good as they taste. Serve with a cocktail that complements the delicate flavours of the cupcake and you've got a perfect treat.

If you're throwing a party, a cupcake and cocktail-inspired theme will allow you to break out the glam without breaking the bank. Keep it simple by choosing one or two signature drinks instead of trying to mix a full bar to order. Start by choosing a theme – anything from tropical luau to retro chic – and then plan your food, drinks, decor and music or other entertainment to match.

Martini

INGREDIENTS
serves 1
3 measures gin
1 tsp dry vermouth,
   or to taste
cocktail olive, to decorate

METHOD
1 Put cracked ice into a
cocktail shaker.

2 Pour the gin and vermouth
over the ice.

3 Shake until well frosted.
Sieve into a chilled
cocktail glass.

4 Decorate with the olive.

Apple Martini

INGREDIENTS
serves 1

1 measure vodka
1 measure sour apple
    schnapps
1 measure apple juice

METHOD

1 Put cracked ice into a cocktail shaker and pour in the vodka, schnapps and apple juice.

2 Shake vigorously until well frosted.

3 Sieve into a chilled cocktail glass.

Caramel Appletini Cupcakes

INGREDIENTS
makes 12

185 g/6½ oz plain flour
1½ tsp baking powder
1 tsp ground ginger
1 tsp ground cinnamon
⅛ tsp ground nutmeg
¼ tsp salt
115 g/4 oz unsalted butter,
    softened
200 g/7 oz caster sugar
1 tsp vanilla extract
2 large eggs
4 tbsp apple sauce
2 tbsp apple juice
2 tbsp apple-flavoured vodka

icing

115 g/4 oz unsalted butter,
    softened
225 g/8 oz soft dark brown sugar
5 tbsp double cream
pinch of salt
2 tbsp apple-flavoured vodka
185–250 g/6½–9 oz icing sugar
    (see method)

to decorate

green food colouring
55 g/2 oz marzipan
25 g/1 oz brown ready-to-roll
    fondant icing

METHOD

1 Preheat the oven to 180°C/350°F/Gas Mark 4 and line a 12-hole cupcake tin with paper cases.

2 Sift together the flour, baking powder, ginger, cinnamon, nutmeg and salt in a bowl. Put the butter and sugar into a separate bowl and whisk until pale and fluffy. Add the vanilla extract, then add the eggs, one at a time, whisking after each addition. Add half of the flour mixture and the apple sauce, apple juice and vodka and whisk well. Add the remaining flour mixture and mix.

3 Spoon the batter into the paper cases and bake in the preheated oven for 20 minutes until a cocktail stick inserted into the centre of a cupcake comes out clean. Leave to cool in the tin for 1–2 minutes, then transfer to a wire rack to cool completely.

4 To make the icing, first make a caramel sauce by melting the butter in a small saucepan over a medium heat. Add the brown sugar, cream and salt and cook, stirring constantly, for about 4 minutes until the sugar has fully dissolved. Remove from the heat, stir in the vodka and set aside to cool for 30 minutes.

5 Pour the caramel sauce into a mixing bowl, reserving 125 ml/4 fl oz to decorate the cupcakes. Add 185 g/6½ oz of the icing sugar to the mixing bowl and whisk until fully incorporated. Add more icing sugar as needed to achieve a piping consistency. Spoon the icing into a piping bag fitted with a star-shaped nozzle and pipe on to the cupcakes.

6 To make the marzipan apple decorations, add a couple of drops of food colouring to the marzipan and knead until the colour is evenly incorporated. Roll the marzipan into 12 balls. Pinch off a small amount of fondant icing and shape into an apple stalk. Press into the top of a marzipan ball and repeat for the 11 remaining balls. To serve, drizzle the cupcakes with the reserved caramel sauce and place a marzipan apple on top of each.

Perfect with
a margarita
cupcake!

Margarita

INGREDIENTS
serves 1
2 lime wedges
rock salt
3 measures white tequila
1 measure Triple Sec or
    Cointreau
1 measures lime juice

METHOD
1 Rub the rim of a chilled cocktail glass with a lime wedge, then dip in a saucer of rock salt to frost.

2 Put cracked ice into a cocktail shaker. Pour the tequila, triple sec or orange-flavoured liqueur and lime juice over the ice. Shake vigorously until frosted.

3 Sieve into the glass and dress with a lime wedge.

Margarita Cupcakes

INGREDIENTS
makes 12

185 g/6½ oz plain flour
1½ tsp baking powder
¼ tsp salt
115 g/4 oz unsalted butter,
   softened
200 g/7 oz caster sugar

2 tsp vanilla extract
2 large eggs
5 tbsp milk
3 tbsp tequila
juice and finely grated
   zest of 1 lime

icing

3 large egg whites
150 g/5½ oz caster sugar
225 g/8 oz unsalted butter,
   softened
4 tbsp triple sec
zest of 1 lime
green food colouring

METHOD

1 Preheat the oven to 180°C/350°F/Gas Mark 4 and line a 12-hole cupcake tin with paper cases.

2 Sift together the flour, baking powder and salt into a bowl. Put the butter and sugar into a separate bowl and whisk until pale and fluffy. Add the vanilla extract and the eggs, one at a time, whisking after each addition. Add half of the flour mixture and the milk, tequila and lime zest and juice and whisk until combined. Add the remaining flour mixture and mix.

3 Spoon the mixture into the paper cases and bake in the preheated oven for 20 minutes until a cocktail stick inserted into the centre of a cupcake comes out clean. Leave to cool in the tin for 1–2 minutes, then transfer to a wire rack to cool completely.

4 To make the icing, put the egg whites and sugar in a heatproof bowl set over a saucepan of gently simmering water and whisk over simmering water until the sugar has completely dissolved. Remove from the heat and whisk the mixture for 4–5 minutes. Add the butter, 2 tablespoons at a time, and continue to whisk until the mixture holds stiff peaks. Add the triple sec, lime zest and 2 drops of food colouring and stir until just combined.

5 Spoon the icing into a piping bag fitted with a star-shaped nozzle and pipe on to the cupcakes.

Daiquiri

INGREDIENTS
serves 1
2 measures white rum
¾ measure lime juice
½ tsp caster sugar dissolved in
    1 tbsp boiling water

METHOD
1 Put cracked ice into a
cocktail shaker. Pour the
ingredients over the ice.
Shake vigorously until
well frosted.

2 Sieve into a chilled
cocktail glass.

Frozen Pineapple Daiquiri

INGREDIENTS
serves 1
2 measures white rum
1 measure lime juice
½ tsp pineapple syrup
55 g/2 oz pineapple, finely
    chopped
pineapple wedges, to decorate

METHOD
1 Mix crushed ice in a blender with the other ingredients until slushy. Pour into a chilled cocktail glass. Dress with some pineapple wedges.

Raspberry Daiquiri Cupcakes

INGREDIENTS
makes 12

185 g/6½ oz self-raising flour
¼ tsp salt
115 g/4 oz unsalted butter,
   softened
200 g/7 oz caster sugar
2 large eggs
125 ml/4 fl oz milk
2 tbsp rum
finely grated zest and juice
   of 1 lime

filling
350 g/12 oz fresh raspberries,
   puréed
55 g/2 oz caster sugar
2 tbsp rum
1 tbsp cornflour

icing
115 g/4 oz unsalted butter,
   softened
250–375 g/9–13 oz icing sugar
   (see method)
1 tsp raspberry extract
2 tbsp double cream
pinch of salt
pink sugar crystals, to decorate

METHOD

1 Preheat the oven to 180°C/350°F/Gas Mark 4 and line a 12-hole cupcake tin with paper cases.

2 Sift together the flour and salt in a bowl. Put the butter and sugar into a separate bowl and whisk until pale and fluffy. Add the eggs, one at a time, whisking after each addition. Add half of the flour mixture, the milk, rum and lime zest and juice and whisk until incorporated. Add the remaining flour mixture and mix.

3 Spoon the mixture into the paper cases and bake in the preheated oven for 20 minutes until a cocktail stick inserted in the centre of a cupcake comes out clean. Leave to cool in the tin for 1–2 minutes, then transfer to a wire rack to cool completely.

4 To make the filling, put the raspberry purée and sugar into a saucepan and bring to the boil, stirring frequently. Put the rum and cornflour into a jug and whisk together. Pour into the boiling raspberry mixture and cook for a further 1–2 minutes, stirring, until the mixture thickens. Remove from the heat and cool, then chill.

5 To make the icing, use an electric mixer to beat the butter until pale and creamy. Add 250g/9 oz of the icing sugar and the remaining ingredients (except the sugar crystals) and 2 tablespoons of the raspberry filling. Whisk until well combined. Add more icing sugar if necessary to achieve a piping consistency. Spoon the icing into a piping bag fitted with a star-shaped nozzle.

6 Use an apple corer to remove the centre of each cupcake and spoon the raspberry filling into each hole. Pipe the icing on to the cupcakes, then sprinkle with the sugar crystals to serve.

When thinking about pairing cupcakes and cocktails, whatever the occasion, there are certain themes that will always be a hit. Summertime begs for the bright flavours of fruit and light, refreshing, citrusy cocktails, while winter nights call for warming flavours like cinnamon in a cocktail such as a Caramel Appletini. Likewise, if you're dreaming of making an escape to a warm, sunny Caribbean island, tropical cocktails and Latin flavours, such as a minty Mojito paired with Coconut & Pineapple Macaroons, would be just the thing to transport you there.

A further way to approach pairing is to match flavour profiles. The citrus notes of a Sidecar or Singapore Sling will echo the citrus notes in the Lemon & White Chocolate Creams, while the white chocolate adds a luxuriously rich base. The bracing sour and bitter notes of a Cosmopolitan are a great foil for sweet and tangy Limoncello Cupcakes.

And, of course, we can't leave out the classic pairing of chocolate and strawberries. A Strawberrini or Strawberry Colada would both be a perfect match for our Chocolate & Pink Peppercorn Cupcakes. Or pair a Chocolate Martini or Chocolate Diva with our Strawberry Mimosa Cupcakes.

Whatever your perfect combination is, a sweet cupcake and a well-mixed cocktail will set the tone for a fabulous time.

Cosmopolitan Cupcakes

INGREDIENTS

makes 12

185 g/6½ oz self-raising flour
¼ tsp salt
115 g/4 oz unsalted butter,
    softened
200 g/7 oz caster sugar
1 tsp vanilla extract
2 large eggs
1 tbsp lime juice
1 tsp finely grated
    lime zest
2 tbsp cranberry vodka
1 tbsp triple sec or orange-
    flavoured liqueur
4 tbsp milk
pink food colouring

icing

115 g/4 oz unsalted butter,
    softened
250–300 g/9–10½ oz icing sugar
    (see method)
2 tbsp cranberry vodka
1 tsp vanilla extract
 pink food colouring

to decorate

pink sugar crystals
4 oz marzipan
green gel food colouring
a green edible-ink marker
12 cocktail umbrellas

METHOD

1 Preheat the oven to 180°C/350°F/Gas Mark 4. Line a 12-hole cupcake tin with paper cases.

2 Sift together the flour and salt in a bowl. Put the butter and sugar into a separate bowl and whisk until pale and fluffy. Add the vanilla extract, then add the eggs, one at a time, whisking after each addition. Add the lime juice, lime zest, vodka, triple sec or orange-flavoured liqueur, milk and half of the flour mixture and whisk until combined. Add the remaining flour mixture and mix well. Stir in a few drops of food colouring and whisk until evenly incorporated.

3 Spoon the mixture into the paper cases and bake in the preheated oven for 20 minutes until a cocktail stick inserted into the centre of a cupcake comes out clean. Leave to cool in the tin for 1–2 minutes, then transfer to a wire rack to cool completely.

4 To make the icing, put the butter into a bowl and whisk with an electric whisk until pale and creamy. Add 250 g/9 oz of the icing sugar along with the vodka and vanilla extract. Whisk together until well combined. Add more icing sugar as needed to achieve a piping consistency. Add a few drops of food colouring and mix until evenly incorporated.

5 Spoon the icing into a piping bag fitted with a star-shaped nozzle. Pipe the icing on to the cupcakes and sprinkle with the pink sugar crystals to decorate.

6 To make the lime wedge decorations, divide the marzipan in half. Add a few drops of green food colouring to one half and knead until evenly incorporated. Add more colour if needed, to achieve a dark green colour; this will be used to make the lime zest. Add a couple of drops of green food colouring to the remaining piece of marzipan and knead until evenly incorporated – this will be used to make the inside of the lime wedge, so it should be light green.

7 Divide both marzipan colours into 12 pieces. Take one

piece of light green marzipan and shape into a half-round about 5 mm/ ¼ inch thick. Lightly pinch the flat side of the half-round to make a wedge shape. Flatten a piece of the dark green marzipan and press in place around the curved edge of the light green wedge, trimming as necessary to give the effect of a zest. Repeat with the remaining marzipan to make 12 lime wedges in total. Using the edible-ink marker, draw lines on the lighter green part to represent the inner membranes of a lime wedge. Set aside to dry.

8 To serve, place a lime wedge on top of each cupcake and insert a cocktail umbrella.

Cosmopolitan

INGREDIENTS
serves 1
2 measures vodka
1 measure Triple Sec
1 measure lime juice
1 measure cranberry juice
orange peel strip, to decorate

METHOD

1 Put cracked ice into a cocktail shaker.

2 Pour the liquid ingredients over the ice.

3 Shake vigorously until well frosted.

4 Sieve into a chilled cocktail glass and decorate with the orange peel.

White Cosmopolitan

INGREDIENTS
serves 1

1½ measures Limoncello
½ measure Cointreau
½ measure white cranberry and
    grape juice
dash orange bitters
cranberries, to decorate

METHOD

1 Put cracked ice into a
cocktail shaker. Pour the
limoncello, Cointreau or
orange-flavoured liqueur,
and cranberry and grape
juice over the ice. Shake
vigorously until well frosted.

2 Sieve into a chilled glass.

3 Add the bitters and dress
with the cranberries.

Limoncello Cupcakes

INGREDIENTS
makes 12

185 g/6½ self-raising flour
¼ tsp salt
115 g/4 oz unsalted butter,
    softened
200 g/7 oz caster sugar

2 large eggs
finely grated zest and juice
    of 1 lemon
4 tbsp milk
rainbow hundreds and
    thousands, to decorate

icing
3 large egg whites
150 g/5½ oz caster sugar
225 g/8 oz unsalted butter,
    softened
4 tbsp limoncello
finely grated zest of 1 lemon

METHOD

1 Preheat the oven to 180°C/350°F/Gas Mark 4 and line a 12-hole cupcake tin with paper cases.

2 Sift together the flour and salt in a bowl. Put the butter and sugar into a separate bowl and whisk until pale and fluffy. Add the eggs, one at a time, whisking after each addition. Add half of the flour mixture, the lemon zest and juice and milk and whisk until incorporated. Add the remaining flour mixture and mix.

3 Spoon the mixture into the paper cases and bake in the preheated oven for 20 minutes until a cocktail stick inserted into the centre of a cupcake comes out clean. Remove from the oven and leave to cool in the tin for 1–2 minutes, then transfer to a wire rack to cool completely.

4 To make the icing, put the egg whites and sugar in a heatproof bowl set over a saucepan of gently simmering water and whisk over simmering water until the sugar has completely dissolved. Remove from the heat and whisk the mixture for 4–5 minutes. Add the butter, 2 tablespoons at a time, and continue to whisk until it holds stiff peaks. Add the limoncello and lemon zest and whisk until just combined.

5 Spoon the icing into a piping bag fitted with a star-shaped nozzle and pipe the icing on to the cupcakes. Top with the rainbow hundreds and thousands and serve.

Sidecar

INGREDIENTS
serves 1
2 measures brandy
1 measure triple sec
1 measure lemon juice
orange peel strip,
    to decorate

METHOD
1 Put cracked ice into
a cocktail shaker, then
pour the liquid ingredients
over the ice.

2 Shake vigorously until
well frosted.

3 Sieve into a chilled cocktail
glass and decorate with the
orange peel.

Singapore Sling

INGREDIENTS
serves 1

2 measures gin
1 measure cherry brandy
1 measure lemon juice
1 tsp grenadine
soda water
lime peel strips and cocktail
    cherries, to decorate

METHOD

1 Put cracked ice into a
cocktail shaker, then pour
the gin over the ice.

2 Add the cherry brandy,
lemon juice and grenadine
and shake vigorously until
well frosted.

3 Half-fill a chilled glass with
cracked ice and sieve the
cocktail over it.

4 Top up with soda water
and decorate with the lime
peel and cherries.

Lemon & White Chocolate Creams

INGREDIENTS
makes 12

280 g/10 oz white chocolate,
    roughly chopped
2 tbsp double cream
finely grated rind of 1 lemon
2 tbsp limoncello
55 g/2 oz unsalted butter,
    softened and diced
25 g/1 oz pistachio nuts, finely
    chopped

METHOD

1 Put 115 g/4 oz of the chocolate and all the cream in a heatproof bowl set over a saucepan of gently simmering water and heat until melted.

2 Remove from the heat, add the lemon rind, limoncello and butter and whisk for 3–4 minutes or until thickened. Transfer to an airtight container and chill in the refrigerator for 6–8 hours or until firm.

3 Line a baking tray with non-stick baking paper. Scoop teaspoonfuls of the mixture and, using the palms of your hands, roll them into truffle-sized balls. Place the balls on the prepared baking tray, cover with clingfilm and freeze for 6–8 hours.

4 Put the remaining chocolate in a heatproof bowl set over a saucepan of gently simmering water and heat until melted. Using two forks, dip each truffle into the chocolate to coat evenly. Return them to the prepared baking tray, sprinkle the pistachios over them and chill in the refrigerator for 1–2 hours or until firm. Store in an airtight container in the refrigerator for up to 5 days.

Your cupcakes and icing can be made ahead of time. Store both the un-iced cupcakes and the icing covered in the refrigerator for up to 3 days. Ice the cupcakes up to 8 hours before party time and store them at room temperature.

If you've whipped up a batch of cupcakes for yourself, rest assured that you don't have to eat them all in one go! Put them into the freezer and you'll have them ready for a treat any time you like. To freeze, wrap un-iced cupcakes in clingfilm or in a resealable, freezerproof plastic bag, and freeze for up to 3 months. To defrost, unwrap the cupcakes and leave them to thaw at room temperature for about an hour.

Most icings, too, can be frozen. Freeze them in a resealable, freezerproof bag and defrost by placing them in the refrigerator for a few hours. Knead the bag to soften the icing if necessary, then spread on your cupcakes or transfer to a piping bag for piping.

Many of your drink ingredients and garnishes can be prepped ahead of time too. For instance, you can peel, slice or dice fruits and make a simple syrup infused with herbs or other flavours well before you need them, whether for a party or to whip up a quick drink for yourself. Many cocktails can be premixed in large batches, stored in jugs in the refrigerator and then poured over ice or whizzed in a blender just before serving.

Long Island Iced Tea

INGREDIENTS
serves 1
2 measures vodka
1 measure gin
1 measure white tequila
1 measure white rum
½ measure white crème de
    menthe
2 measures lemon juice
1 tsp sugar syrup
cola
lime wedge, to decorate

METHOD
1 Put cracked ice into a cocktail shaker. Pour all the liquid ingredients except the cola over the ice, add the sugar and shake vigorously until well frosted.

2 Half-fill a tall glass with cracked ice and sieve the cocktail over the ice.

3 Top up with cola.

4 Decorate with the lime wedge.

Manhattan

INGREDIENTS

serves 1
dash Angostura bitters
3 measures rye whiskey
1 measure sweet vermouth
cocktail cherry, to decorate

METHOD

1 Put cracked ice into a cocktail shaker.

2 Pour the liquid ingredients over the ice.

3 Shake vigorously until well frosted.

4 Sieve into a chilled cocktail glass and decorate with the cherry.

Malibu Bay Cupcakes

INGREDIENTS
makes 12

125 ml/4 fl oz cranberry juice
200 g/7 oz plus 2 tbsp caster
    sugar
185 g/6½ oz self-raising flour
¼ tsp salt
115 g/4 oz unsalted butter,
    softened
2 large eggs
100 ml/3½ fl oz coconut milk
2 tbsp white rum
2 tbsp chopped dried
    cranberries

icing

3 large egg whites
150 g/5½ oz caster sugar
225 g/8 oz unsalted butter,
    softened
3 tbsp white rum
1 tbsp coconut extract

to decorate

35 g/1¼ oz desiccated coconut
pink food colouring
12 cocktail straws

METHOD

1 Preheat the oven to 180°C/350°F/Gas Mark 4 and line a 12-hole cupcake tin with paper cases.

2 Combine the cranberry juice and the 2 tablespoons of the sugar in a small saucepan and bring to the boil over a medium–high heat. Boil for about 10 minutes until reduced to about 2 tablespoons. Set aside to cool.

3 Sift together the flour and salt in a bowl. Put the butter and remaining sugar into a separate bowl and whisk until pale and fluffy. Add the eggs, one at a time, whisking after each addition. Add half the flour mixture, the cranberry reduction, coconut milk and rum, and whisk until incorporated. Add the remaining flour mixture and mix. Stir in the dried cranberries.

4 Spoon the mixture into the paper cases. Bake for 20 minutes until a cocktail stick inserted into a cupcake comes out clean. Cool in the tin for 1–2 minutes, then transfer to a wire rack to cool completely.

5 For the icing, put the egg whites and sugar in a heatproof bowl set over a saucepan of gently simmering water and whisk over simmering water until the sugar has completely dissolved. Remove from the heat and whisk for 4–5 minutes. Add the butter, 25 g/1 oz at a time, and whisk until it holds stiff peaks. Add the rum and coconut extract and whisk until just combined. Spoon the icing into a piping bag fitted with a star-shaped nozzle. Pipe on to the cupcakes.

6 To decorate, combine the coconut with a few drops of the food colouring and mix until the colour is evenly distributed. Scatter over the iced cupcakes and insert a cocktail straw into each.

Miami Beach

INGREDIENTS
serves 1
2 measures Scotch whisky
1½ measures dry vermouth
2 measures pink grapefruit juice
orange peel strip, to decorate

METHOD
1 Put cracked ice into a cocktail shaker.

2 Pour the whisky, vermouth and grapefruit juice over the ice.

3 Shake vigorously until well frosted. Sieve into a chilled cocktail glass.

4 Decorate with the orange peel strip.

Club Mojito

INGREDIENTS
serves 1
1 tsp sugar syrup
6 fresh mint leaves, plus extra
    to decorate
juice of ½ lime
2 measures Jamaican rum
soda water
dash Angostura bitters

METHOD
1 Put the sugar syrup, mint leaves and lime juice into an old-fashioned glass.

2 Lightly crush the mint leaves, then fill the glass with cracked ice and pour the rum over it.

3 Top up with soda water.

4 Finish with the Angostura bitters and decorate with the remaining mint leaves.

Coconut & Pineapple Macaroons

INGREDIENTS
makes 16
55 g/2 oz ground almonds
15 g/½ oz finely ground
   desiccated coconut,
   plus 2 tbsp toasted,
   to decorate
115 g/4 oz icing sugar
2 large egg whites
55 g/2 oz caster sugar

filling
55 g/2 oz unsalted butter,
   softened
2 tsp pineapple juice
115 g/4 oz icing sugar, sifted
2 rings canned pineapple,
   drained and finely chopped

METHOD

1 Put the ground almonds, ground coconut and icing sugar into a food processor and whizz for 15 seconds. Sift the mixture into a bowl. Line two baking trays with baking paper.

2 Put the egg whites into a large bowl and whip until holding soft peaks. Gradually whisk in the caster sugar until you have a firm, glossy meringue.

3 Using a palette knife, fold the almond mixture into the meringue one third at a time. When all the dry ingredients are thoroughly incorporated, continue to cut and fold the mixture until it forms a shiny mixture with a thick, ribbon-like consistency.

4 Pour the mixture into a piping bag fitted with a 1-cm/ ½-inch plain nozzle. Pipe 32 small rounds on to the prepared baking trays. Tap the baking trays firmly on to a work surface to remove air bubbles. Sprinkle over the toasted coconut. Leave to stand at room temperature for 30 minutes. Preheat the oven to 160°C/325°F/Gas Mark 3.

5 Bake in the preheated oven for 10–15 minutes. Leave to cool for 10 minutes. Carefully peel the macaroons off the baking paper and leave to cool completely.

6 To make the filling, whisk the butter and pineapple juice in a bowl until pale and fluffy. Gradually whisk in the icing sugar until smooth and creamy, then fold in the chopped pineapple. Use to sandwich pairs of macaroons together.

Sex on the Beach

INGREDIENTS
serves 1

1 measure peach schnapps
1 measure vodka
2 measures fresh orange juice
3 measures cranberry and
    peach juice
dash lemon juice
piece of orange peel, to
    decorate

METHOD

1 Put cracked ice into a cocktail shaker. Pour the liquid ingredients, except the lemon juice, over the ice. Shake vigorously until well frosted.

2 Sieve into a glass filled with crushed ice and splash the lemon juice over the top.

3 Dress with the orange peel.

Mai Tai

INGREDIENTS
serves 1
2 measures white rum
2 measures dark rum
1 measure orange curaçao
1 measure lime juice
1 tbsp orgeat syrup
1 tbsp grenadine
pineapple wedges, cocktail
   cherries and thinly pared
   orange peel, to decorate

METHOD
1 Put cracked ice into a cocktail shaker. Pour the liquid ingredients over the ice. Shake vigorously until well frosted.

2 Sieve into a chilled cocktail glass and dress with pineapple wedges, cocktail cherries and orange peel.

Fabulous Food
for Friends

Having a glamorous gathering for your friends can be as simple as baking up a batch of cupcakes and giving the old cocktail shaker a shake. Pick a theme and let your food and drink pairing follow suit.

For holiday parties go for a Strawberrini paired with Chocolate & Pink Peppercorn Cupcakes. Celebrate your best friend's birthday with an indulgent chocolate theme – Chocolate Diva paired with Chilli Chocolate Cupcakes. Pina Colada served with Pina Colada Cupcakes are perfect for a barbecue or a summer evening get-together. If you're looking to create a refreshing and rejuvenating atmosphere, host a 'spa day' and serve non-alcoholic cucumber refreshers with antioxidant-rich green tea along with pomegranate cupcakes.

Happiness is an iced cupcake with a cherry on top!

Pink Lemon Meringue Cupcakes

INGREDIENTS
makes 12
185 g/6½ oz self-raising flour
¼ tsp salt
115 g/4 oz unsalted butter,
    softened
200 g/7 oz caster sugar
1 tsp vanilla extract
2 large eggs
finely grated zest and juice
    of 1 lemon
4 tbsp milk
pink food colouring

filling
225 g/8 oz lemon curd
125 ml/4 fl oz double cream,
    whipped

icing
4 large egg whites
200 g/7 oz caster sugar
¼ tsp cream of tartar
1 tbsp lemon juice
1 tsp lemon extract
pink food colouring, optional

METHOD
1 Preheat the oven to 180°C/350°F/Gas Mark 4 and line a 12-hole cupcake tin with paper cases.

2 Sift together the flour and salt in a bowl. Put the butter and sugar into a separate bowl and whisk until pale and fluffy. Add the vanilla extract, then add the eggs, one at a time, whisking after each addition. Add half of the flour mixture, the lemon zest and juice and milk, and whisk until combined. Add the remaining flour mixture and mix. Add a few drops of food colouring and stir until evenly incorporated.

3 Spoon the mixture into the paper cases and bake in the preheated oven for 20 minutes until a cocktail stick inserted into the centre of a cupcake comes out clean. Leave to cool in the tin for 1–2 minutes, then transfer to a wire rack to cool completely.

4 To make the filling, gently fold the lemon curd into the whipped cream and chill until ready to use.

5 Use an apple corer to remove the centre of each cupcake. Spoon the lemon curd filling into the holes.

6 To make the icing, put the egg whites, sugar and cream of tartar in a heatproof bowl set over a saucepan of gently simmering water and whisk over simmering water until the sugar has completely dissolved. Remove from the heat and whisk the mixture for 4–5 minutes until it holds stiff peaks. Add the lemon juice, lemon extract and a few drops of food colouring if using, and whisk until combined.

7 Spoon the icing into a piping bag fitted with a large round nozzle and pipe on to the cupcakes.

Strawberrini

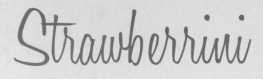

INGREDIENTS
serves 1
6 fresh or frozen strawberries
1 tbsp icing sugar
splash lime juice
splash fraise liqueur
2 measures vodka, well iced

METHOD

1 Reserve one or two strawberries to add later.

2 Crush the remaining strawberries in a bowl with the sugar, lime juice and fraise liqueur. Sieve well.

3 Pour the vodka into a chilled martini glass and add the purée. Dress with the reserved strawberries.

Woo Woo

INGREDIENTS
serves 1
4 measures cranberry juice
2 measures vodka
2 measures peach schnapps

METHOD
1 Half-fill a chilled cocktail glass with crushed ice.

2 Pour the cranberry juice over the ice.

3 Add the vodka and peach schnapps.

Chocolate & Pink Peppercorn Cupcakes

INGREDIENTS
makes 12
115 g/4 oz self-raising flour
60 g/2¼ oz cocoa powder
¼ tsp salt
115 g/4 oz unsalted butter,
    softened
200 g/7 oz caster sugar
2 tsp vanilla extract
2 large eggs
100 ml/3½ fl oz soured cream
1 tbsp pink peppercorns,
    crushed, to decorate

icing
4 tbsp milk
1 tbsp pink peppercorns,
    crushed
115 g/4 oz unsalted butter,
    softened
250–300 g/9–10½ oz icing sugar
    (see method)
2 tsp vanilla extract

METHOD
1 Preheat the oven to 180°C/350°F/Gas Mark 4 and line a 12-hole cupcake tin with paper cases.

2 Sift together the flour, cocoa powder and salt in a bowl. Put the butter and sugar into a separate bowl and whisk until pale and fluffy. Add the vanilla extract, then add the eggs one at a time, whisking after each addition. Add half of the flour mixture and the soured cream and whisk until combined. Add the remaining flour mixture and mix.

3 Spoon the mixture into the paper cases and bake in the preheated oven for 20 minutes until a cocktail stick inserted into the centre of a cupcake comes out clean. Leave to cool in the tin for 1–2 minutes, then transfer to a wire rack to cool completely.

4 To make the icing, put the milk and peppercorns into a small saucepan and heat over a medium heat until just boiling. Reduce the heat to low and simmer for about 5 minutes, stirring frequently. Sieve the milk into a bowl, discarding the peppercorns, and leave to cool for about 10 minutes.

5 Add the butter, 250 g/9 oz of the icing sugar and the vanilla extract to the milk and whisk, using an electric whisk, until well combined. Add more icing sugar if needed to achieve a piping consistency. Spoon the icing into a piping bag fitted with a star-shaped nozzle and pipe on to the cupcakes.

6 To decorate, sprinkle the crushed pink peppercorns over the tops of the cupcakes.

Pina Colada

INGREDIENTS
serves 1
2 measures white rum
1 measure dark rum
3 measures pineapple juice
2 measures coconut cream
pineapple wedges, to decorate

METHOD
1 Put crushed ice into a blender with the white rum, dark rum, pineapple juice and creamed coconut and process until smooth.

2 Pour, without sieving, into a chilled tall glass and dress with the pineapple wedges.

Strawberry Colada

INGREDIENTS
serves 1
3 measures golden rum
4 measures pineapple juice
1 measure coconut cream
6 strawberries, hulled
pineapple wedge and halved
    strawberry, to decorate

METHOD
1 Put crushed ice into a
blender with the rum,
pineapple juice and
creamed coconut.

2 Add the strawberries
to the blender. Whizz until
smooth.

3 Pour, without sieving, into a
tall chilled glass. Decorate
with the pineapple wedge
and strawberry.

Pina Colada Cupcakes

INGREDIENTS
makes 12

185 g/6½ oz self-raising flour
¼ tsp salt
115 g/4 oz unsalted butter,
    softened
200 g/7 oz caster sugar
2 large eggs
2 tbsp white rum
125 ml/4 oz milk
100 g/3½ oz crushed canned
    pineapple in juice, drained
55 g/2 oz desiccated coconut
12 cocktail umbrellas,
    to decorate

icing

4 large egg whites
200 g/7 oz caster sugar
¼ tsp cream of tartar
1 tbsp coconut extract
2 tbsp double cream

METHOD

1 Preheat the oven to 180°C/350°F/Gas Mark 4. Line a 12-hole cupcake tin with paper cases.

2 Sift together the flour and salt in a bowl. Put the butter and sugar into a separate bowl and whisk until pale and fluffy. Add the eggs one at a time, whisking after each addition. Add the rum, milk and half of the flour mixture and mix until combined. Add the remaining flour mixture and mix thoroughly. Stir in the pineapple.

3 Spoon the mixture into the paper cases and bake in the preheated oven for 20 minutes until a cocktail stick inserted into the centre of a cupcake comes out clean. Leave to cool in the tin for 1–2 minutes, then transfer to a wire rack to cool completely. Keep the oven on.

4 To toast the coconut, line a baking tray with foil and spread the coconut out on it. Bake, tossing halfway through, for about 6–8 minutes until a golden colour. Remove from the oven and leave to cool.

5 To make the icing, put the egg whites, sugar and cream of tartar in a heatproof bowl set over a saucepan of gently simmering water and whisk until the sugar has completely dissolved. Remove from the heat and whisk the mixture for 4–5 minutes or until it holds stiff peaks. Add the coconut extract and double cream and stir until just combined. Spoon the icing into a piping bag fitted with a star-shaped nozzle and pipe on to the cupcakes.

6 Sprinkle with the toasted coconut and decorate each cupcake with a cocktail umbrella.

Tips for baking success!

CHOOSING INGREDIENTS

Only the most basic ingredients available at your regular supermarket are needed to make fantastic cupcakes. As cupcakes rely on so few ingredients, it's a good idea to splurge for the best quality you can find. From butter (we use unsalted) and eggs to flour (our recipes call for self-raising or plain) and sugar (for cake mixture, look for caster sugar), every ingredient is best when it is of the highest quality and used before its 'best before' date.

GETTING STARTED

For the best results, butter, eggs, milk, cream and other refrigerated ingredients should be brought to room temperature before baking. This helps to ensure your cakes have a tender texture.

MEASURING

Always use either metric or imperial measures – do not switch between the two. Accurate kitchen scales are essential for the best results. Measure liquids in a liquid measuring jug at eye level. To measure dry ingredients in measuring spoons, scoop the ingredient with the spoon and level it off with the flat edge of a rounded knife.

MIXING

Mixing may seem like a no-brainer, but there is a technique to it. Butter and sugar should be well creamed together. This takes about 3 minutes using an electric whisk set on medium speed. Keep creaming until the mixture is light and fluffy. Once the eggs and flour have been added, however, mix only as long as necessary to completely incorporate them without overworking your mixture. Also take care to scrape down the base and sides of the mixing bowl with a rubber palette knife frequently between additions to ensure that all of the ingredients are well mixed.

BAKING AND ICING

Always preheat the oven for at least 15 minutes. Scoop your mixture into a cupcake tin lined with paper cases. Fill each case about two-thirds full to produce a nice, dome-shaped cupcake that will provide the perfect blank canvas for decorating. Avoid overcooking your cupcakes by checking for doneness a minute or two before the recommended cooking time is up. A wooden cocktail stick or metal skewer inserted into the centre of a cupcake should come out clean. When finished, remove from the oven promptly and leave the cupcakes to cool in the tin for just a minute or two, until they are cool enough to handle. Using a palette knife or small knife, lift the cupcakes (in their cases) from the tin and transfer to a wire rack to cool completely.

Always cool cupcakes completely before icing. Once they're cooled, it's time to get artsy with the icing, hundreds and thousands and other decorations. Have fun decorating your little cakes and you'll set the tone for a fun-filled party.

Skinny Strawberry Fizz Cocktail

INGREDIENTS
serves 4

200 g/7 oz strawberries, hulled
2 tbsp agave syrup
juice of 1 lime
100 ml/3½ fl oz vodka
400 ml/14 fl oz diet cola
whole strawberries and strips of
    lime zest, to decorate

METHOD

1 Put the strawberries, syrup
and lime juice in a plastic
jug and whizz with a stick
blender or in a food
processor until smooth.

2 Add crushed ice to each
of 4 tall glasses.

3 Pour the strawberry mixture
evenly into each glass, add
1 measure of vodka to each
glass and stir to mix.

4 Top up the glasses with
the cola to taste and place
a strawberry and lime peel
twist on the rims.

Skinny Apricot Refresher

INGREDIENTS
serves 2
6 apricots
1 orange
1 fresh lemongrass stalk
2-cm/¾-inch piece fresh ginger,
   peeled

METHOD
1 Halve and stone the apricots. Peel the orange, leaving some of the white pith. Cut the lemongrass into chunks.

2 Place the apricots, orange, lemongrass and ginger in a juicer and juice together all the ingredients. Pour the mixture into glasses, add ice cubes and serve.

Who says treats have to be indulgent!

SKINNY

Skinny Mini Muffins

INGREDIENTS
makes 48

185 g/6½ oz self-raising flour
1½ tsp baking powder
70 g/2½ oz soft light brown sugar
100 g/3½ oz dried cranberries
25 g/1 oz mini marshmallows
finely grated rind of
   ½ small lemon
1 tbsp lemon juice
1 egg, beaten
125 ml/4 floz skimmed milk
3 tbsp sunflower oil
½ tsp vanilla extract

METHOD

1 Preheat the oven to
200°C/400°F/Gas Mark 6.
Put 48 paper cases on 2 or
3 baking sheets or in mini-
muffin tins.

2 Sift the flour and baking
powder into a bowl and
add the sugar. Stir in the
cranberries and
marshmallows.

3 Whisk together lemon rind
and juice, egg, milk, oil and
vanilla in a bowl, then stir into
the dry ingredients to make
a soft mixture.

4 Spoon the mixture into
the paper cases and bake
in the preheated oven for
12–15 minutes or until risen,
firm and golden. Transfer
to a wire rack to cool
before serving.

Watermelon Cupcakes

INGREDIENTS
makes 12
185 g/6½ oz self-raising flour
¼ tsp salt
115 g/4 oz unsalted butter,
    softened
200 g/7 oz caster sugar
2 tsp vanilla extract
2 large eggs
125 ml/4 fl oz milk
pink food colouring
85 g/3 oz mini plain chocolate
    chips

icing
115 g/4 oz unsalted butter,
    softened
250–300 g/9–10½ oz icing sugar
    (see method)
1 tablepoon milk
1 tsp vanilla extract
pinch of salt
green food colouring

METHOD
1 Preheat the oven to 180°C/350°F/Gas Mark 4 and line a 12-hole cupcake tin with paper cases.

2 Sift together the flour and salt in a bowl. Put the butter and sugar into a separate bowl and whisk until pale and fluffy. Add the vanilla extract, then add the eggs one at a time, whisking after each addition. Add half of the flour mixture and the milk and whisk until incorporated. Add the remaining flour mixture and mix. Add several drops of food colouring and whisk until evenly combined. Gradually add more colouring until a vibrant pink is achieved. Stir in the chocolate chips.

3 Spoon the mixture into the paper cases and bake in the preheated oven for 20 minutes until a cocktail stick inserted into the centre of a cupcake comes out clean. Leave to cool in the tin for 1–2 minutes, then transfer to a wire rack to cool completely.

4 To make the icing, put the butter, 250 g/9 oz of the icing sugar, the milk, vanilla extract and salt into a bowl and whisk with an electric whisk until well combined. Add more icing sugar if needed, to achieve a piping consistency. Add several drops of food colouring and whisk until evenly incorporated. Gradually add more colouring until a dark green colour is achieved. Transfer the icing to a piping bag fitted with a star-shaped nozzle and pipe on to the cupcakes.

Cucumber Refresher

INGREDIENTS
serves 1
2–3 fresh mint sprigs
1 tsp icing sugar
juice of 1 lime
2.5-cm/1-inch piece cucumber,
    thinly sliced
sparkling water, chilled

METHOD
1 Remove the leaves from the mint sprigs and chop finely. Mix half of the chopped mint with the sugar on a saucer.

2 Rub a little of the lime juice around the rim of a wine glass and dip in the minted sugar to frost.

3 Put the remaining lime juice and chopped mint into the prepared glass with the cucumber and cracked ice. Top up with chilled sparkling water.

Rum Cooler

INGREDIENTS
serves 1
1½ measures white rum
1½ measures pineapple juice
1 banana, peeled and sliced
juice of 1 lime
lime peel twist, to decorate

METHOD
1 Put ice, rum, pineapple juice and banana into a blender.

2 Add the lime juice and whizz for about 1 minute or until smooth.

3 Fill a chilled glass with cracked ice and pour the cocktail over the ice.

4 Decorate with the lime peel.

Pomegranate & Green Tea Cupcakes

INGREDIENTS
makes 12
185 g/6½ oz self-raising flour
1 tbsp green tea (matcha)
    powder
¼ tsp salt
115 g/4 oz unsalted butter,
    softened
200 g/7 oz caster sugar
1 tsp vanilla extract
2 large eggs
4 tbsp milk
40 g/1½ oz pomegranate seeds,
    to decorate

pomegranate syrup
500 ml/18 fl oz pomegranate
    juice
100 g/3½ oz caster sugar

icing
115 g/4 oz unsalted butter,
    softened
185–250 g/6½–9 oz icing sugar
    (see method)

METHOD
1 To make the pomegranate syrup, put the pomegranate juice and sugar into a saucepan and bring to the boil over a medium–high heat, stirring occasionally, until the sugar has dissolved. Reduce the heat to low and cook until the mixture has reduced to about 125 ml/4 fl oz. Set aside to cool.

2 Preheat the oven to 180°C/350°F/Gas Mark 4. Line a 12-hole cupcake tin with paper cases.

3 Sift together the flour, green tea powder and salt in a bowl. Put the butter and sugar into a separate bowl and whisk until pale and fluffy. Add the vanilla extract, then add the eggs one at a time, whisking after each addition. Add half of the flour mixture, 4 tablespoons of the pomegranate syrup and the milk and mix to incorporate. Add the remaining flour mixture and mix.

4 Spoon the mixture into the paper cases and bake in the preheated oven for 20 minutes or until a cocktail stick inserted into the centre of a cupcake comes out clean. Leave to cool in the tin for 1–2 minutes, then transfer to a wire rack to cool completely.

5 To make the icing, put the butter, 185 g/6½ oz icing sugar and the remaining pomegranate syrup in a bowl and whisk with an electric whisk until well combined. Add more icing sugar if needed to achieve a piping consistency. Spoon the icing into a piping bag fitted with a star-shaped nozzle and pipe on to the cupcakes.

6 To decorate, sprinkle the pomegranate seeds over the cupcakes.

Vanilla Chai Tea Cupcakes

INGREDIENTS
makes 12
125 ml/4 fl oz milk
3 chai teabags
185 g/6½ oz self-raising flour
1 tsp mixed spice
¼ tsp salt
115 g/4 oz unsalted butter,
    softened
200 g/7 oz caster sugar
1 tbsp vanilla extract
2 large eggs
1 tsp ground cinnamon and
    1 tbsp sugar, mixed, to
    decorate

icing
3 large egg whites
150 g/5½ oz caster sugar
225 g/8 oz unsalted butter,
    softened
1 tsp vanilla extract
1 tsp ground cinnamon

METHOD
1 Preheat the oven to 180°C/350°F/Gas Mark 4 and line a 12-hole cupcake tin with paper cases.

2 Heat the milk in a small saucepan until just boiling. Add the teabags, remove from the heat and let infuse for 15 minutes. Remove and discard the teabags and set the milk aside to cool completely.

3 Sift together the flour, mixed spice and salt in a bowl. Put the butter and sugar into a separate bowl and whisk until pale and fluffy. Add the vanilla extract, then add the eggs one at a time, whisking after each addition, until combined. Add half of the flour mixture and the tea-infused milk and whisk until combined. Add the remaining flour and mix.

4 Spoon the mixture into the paper cases and bake in the preheated oven for 20 minutes until a cocktail stick inserted into the centre of a cupcake comes out clean. Remove from the oven, leave to cool in the tin for 1–2 minutes, then transfer to a wire rack to cool completely.

5 To make the icing, put the egg whites and sugar in a heatproof bowl set over a saucepan of gently simmering water and whisk until the sugar has completely dissolved. Remove from the heat and whisk for 4–5 minutes. Add the butter 25 g/1 oz at a time, and whisk until it holds stiff peaks. Add the vanilla extract and cinnamon and whisk until just combined. Spoon the icing into a piping bag fitted with a star-shaped nozzle and pipe on to the cupcakes.

6 To decorate, scatter the cinnamon sugar over the cupcakes.

With chocolate and friends, you can conquer just about anything!

Devil's Food Chocolate Cupcakes

INGREDIENTS
makes 18

55 g/2 oz soft margarine
100 g/3½ oz soft light brown
   sugar
2 large eggs
100 g/3½ oz plain flour
½ tsp bicarbonate of soda
25 g/1 oz cocoa powder
125 ml/4 fl oz soured cream

icing

115 g/4 oz plain chocolate,
   broken into pieces
2 tbsp caster sugar
150 ml/5 fl oz soured cream
shaved chocolate curls,
   to decorate

METHOD

1 Preheat the oven to 180°/350°F/Gas Mark 4 and put 18 paper cases in two cupcake tins.

2 Put the margarine, brown sugar, eggs, flour, bicarbonate of soda and cocoa in a large bowl and, using an electric handheld mixer, whisk together until just smooth. Using a metal spoon, fold in the soured cream. Divide the mixture equally between the paper cases and smooth the tops.

3 Bake in the preheated oven for 20 minutes or until well risen and firm to the touch. Transfer to a wire rack to cool.

4 To make the icing, melt the chocolate in a heatproof bowl set over a saucepan of gently simmering water. Cool slightly, then whisk in the sugar and soured cream until combined. Spread the icing over each cake and leave to set in the refrigerator. Serve decorated with chocolate curls.

Chocolate Martini

INGREDIENTS
serves 1
lemon wedge
cocoa powder
2 measures vodka
¼ measure crème de cacao
2 dashes orange flower water

METHOD

1 Rub the rim of a chilled cocktail glass with the lemon wedge, then dip in a saucer of cocoa powder.

2 Put cracked ice into a cocktail shaker. Pour the vodka, crème de cacao and orange flower water over the ice. Shake vigorously until well frosted.

3 Sieve into the glass.

Chocolate Diva

INGREDIENTS
serves 1

115 g/4 oz good-quality milk
    chocolate, melted
1 measure Grand Marnier
1 measure vodka
1 measure crème de cacao
1 tbsp fresh orange juice
fresh edible petals, to decorate

METHOD

1 Mix the melted chocolate
with the Grand Marnier, vodka,
crème de cacao and orange
juice until well blended.

2 Pour into a chilled cocktail
glass and float petals on the
top to decorate.

Chilli Chocolate Cupcakes

INGREDIENTS
makes 12

115 g/4 oz plain flour
60 g/2¼ oz cocoa powder
1½ tsp baking powder
½ tsp ground cinnamon
1 tsp mild chilli powder
¼ tsp cayenne pepper
¼ tsp salt
115 g/4 oz unsalted butter,
   softened
200 g/7oz caster sugar
2 tsp vanilla extract
2 large eggs
125 ml/4 fl oz milk
55 g/2 oz plain chocolate,
   to decorate

icing

115 g/4 oz unsalted butter,
   softened
185–250 g/6½–9 oz icing sugar
   (see method)
25 g/1 oz cocoa powder
2 tbsp milk
1 tsp vanilla extract
1 tsp ground cinnamon

METHOD

1 Preheat the oven to 180°C/350°F/Gas Mark 4 and line a 12-hole cupcake tin with paper cases.

2 Sift together the flour, cocoa powder, baking powder, cinnamon, chilli powder, cayenne pepper and salt in a bowl. Put the butter and sugar into a separate bowl and whisk until pale and fluffy. Add the vanilla extract, then add the eggs one at a time, whisking after each addition. Add half of the flour mixture and the milk and whisk until incorporated. Add the remaining flour mixture and mix.

3 Spoon the mixture into the paper cases and bake in the preheated oven for 20 minutes until risen and a cocktail stick inserted into the centre of a cupcake comes out clean. Leave to cool in the tin for 1–2 minutes, then transfer to a wire rack to cool completely.

4 To make the icing, put the butter in a bowl and whisk with an electric whisk until pale and fluffy. Add 185 g/6½ oz of the icing sugar together with the cocoa powder, milk, vanilla extract and cinnamon. Whisk together until well combined. Add more icing sugar if necessary to achieve a piping consistency. Spoon the icing into a piping bag fitted with a star-shaped nozzle and pipe on to the cupcakes.

5 To decorate, grate the chocolate over the top of the cupcakes.

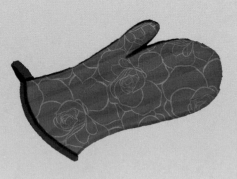

Salted Caramel Cupcakes

INGREDIENTS
makes 12
185 g/6½ oz self-raising flour
¼ tsp salt
115 g/4 oz unsalted butter,
    softened
100 g/3½ oz caster sugar
100 g/3½ soft dark brown sugar
1 tsp vanilla extract
1 tsp coffee extract
2 large eggs
125 ml/4 fl oz milk
1 tsp sea salt flakes,
    to decorate

icing
115 g/4 oz unsalted butter,
    softened
225 g/8 oz dark brown sugar
5 tbsp double cream
½ tsp salt
185–300 g/6½–10½ oz icing
    sugar (see method)

METHOD

1 Preheat the oven to 180°C/350°F/Gas Mark 4 and line a 12-hole cupcake tin with paper cases.

2 Sift together the flour and salt in a bowl. Put the butter, sugar and brown sugar into a separate bowl and cream until fluffy. Add the vanilla extract and coffee extract, then add the eggs one at a time, whisking after each addition. Add half of the flour mixture and the milk and whisk until incorporated. Add the remaining flour mixture and mix well.

3 Spoon the mixture into the paper cases and bake in the preheated oven for 20 minutes until a cocktail stick inserted into the centre of a cupcake comes out clean. Leave to cool in the tin for 1–2 minutes, then transfer to a wire rack to cool completely.

4 To make the icing, first prepare a caramel sauce by melting the butter in a small saucepan over a medium heat. Add the brown sugar, cream and salt and cook, stirring continuously, for about 4 minutes or until the sugar has completely dissolved. Remove from the heat and set aside to cool.

5 Add 185 g/6½ oz of the icing sugar to the caramel sauce and whisk until fully incorporated. Add more icing sugar if needed to achieve a piping consistency. Spoon into a piping bag fitted with a star-shaped nozzle and pipe on to the cupcakes.

6 To decorate, sprinkle the cupcakes with sea salt flakes.

Vanilla Swirl Brownies

INGREDIENTS
makes 12

85 g/3 oz lightly salted butter, plus extra for greasing
115 g/4 oz plain chocolate, roughly chopped
1 egg
1 egg yolk

100 g/3½ oz soft light brown sugar
50 g/1¾ oz plain flour
½ tsp baking powder
85 g/3 oz milk chocolate, roughly chopped

icing

150 g/5½ oz mascarpone cheese
30 g/1 oz icing sugar
1 tsp vanilla extract
milk or plain chocolate curls, to sprinkle

METHOD

1 Preheat the oven to 190°C/375°F/Gas Mark 5 and line a 12-hole cupcake tin with paper cases.

2 Put the butter and plain chocolate in a heatproof bowl set over a saucepan of gently simmering water and heat until melted. Leave the mixture to cool slightly.

3 Put the egg, egg yolk and light brown sugar in a mixing bowl and whisk together with an electric handheld mixer until the mixture begins to turn frothy. Stir in the melted chocolate. Sift the flour and baking powder into the bowl, sprinkle in the milk chocolate and stir together. Using a teaspoon, spoon the mixture into the paper cases.

4 Bake in the preheated oven for 12–15 minutes, or until the brownies feel dry but give a little when gently pressed. (If you're unsure, it's better to slightly undercook brownies because they lose their gooeyness when over-baked.) Leave to cool in the tin for 10 minutes, then transfer to a wire rack to completely cool.

5 For the icing, put the mascarpone cheese, icing sugar and vanilla extract in a small bowl and whisk with an electric handheld mixer until smooth and creamy. Put the mixture in a piping bag fitted with a 1-cm/½-inch star-shaped nozzle and pipe swirls over the cakes. Sprinkle with chocolate curls to decorate.

Celebrate in Style

There is nothing like a tower of beautifully decorated cupcakes or a tray of expertly mixed cocktails to mark a special occasion. Put them together and you are all set to celebrate in style. Whether fêting an engagement, a special anniversary or an important achievement, the perfect cupcake and cocktail pairing is sure to strike just the right note.

Both cupcakes and cocktails offer opportunities for endless creativity. Mixing and matching both flavours and visual elements is key to letting them shine. Pairing them in clever ways only adds to their power to delight.

In their simplest forms, both cupcakes and cocktails set a celebratory tone, but served in fancy glasses rimmed with sparkling decorating sugar or adorned with glittering sprinkles, heart-shaped decorations or candy canes and reindeer, they take your celebration to the next level and create an unbeatable ambience all on their own.

Champagne Cocktail

INGREDIENTS
serves 1
1 sugar cube
2 dashes Angostura bitters
1 measure brandy
champagne, chilled

METHOD
1 Place the sugar cube in the base of a chilled champagne flute with the Angostura bitters.

2 Pour over the brandy and top up slowly with champagne.

Bellini

INGREDIENTS
serves 1
lemon wedge
caster sugar
1 measure peach juice
3 measures champagne,
    chilled

METHOD
1 Rub the rim of a chilled
champagne flute with the
lemon wedge, then dip in
a saucer of sugar to frost.

2 Pour the peach juice into
the prepared glass.

3 Add the chilled
champagne.

Strawberry Mimosa Cupcakes

INGREDIENTS
makes 12
185 g/6½ oz plain flour
¼ tsp salt
115 g/4 oz unsalted butter,
    softened
200 g/7 oz caster sugar
1 tsp vanilla extract
2 eggs
125 ml/4 fl oz champagne or
    other sparkling wine
finely grated zest of 1 orange
2 tbsp orange juice

filling
4 tbsp water
2 tbsp cornflour
175 g/6 oz hulled fresh or frozen
    strawberries, diced
85 g/3 oz caster sugar
4 tbsp champagne or other
    sparkling wine

icing
115 g/4 oz unsalted butter,
    softened
450–500 g/1 lb–1 lb 2oz
    icing sugar (see method)
4 tbsp champagne, or other
    sparkling wine
finely grated zest of 1 orange
2 tbsp orange juice

to decorate
115 g/4 oz marzipan
red food colouring
yellow food colouring
orange edible-ink marker
pink sugar crystals

METHOD

1 Preheat the oven to 180°C/350°F/Gas Mark 4 and line a 12-hole cupcake tin with paper cases.

2 Sift together the flour and salt in a bowl. Put the butter and sugar into a separate bowl and whisk until pale and fluffy. Add the vanilla extract, then add the eggs one at a time, whisking after each addition. Add half of the flour mixture and the champagne and whisk until combined. Add the remaining flour mixture, orange zest and orange juice and mix.

3 Spoon the mixture into the paper cases and bake in the preheated oven for 20 minutes until a cocktail stick inserted into the centre of a cupcake comes out clean. Leave to cool in the tin for 1–2 minutes, then transfer to a wire rack to cool completely.

4 To make the filling, stir the water and cornflour in a saucepan and bring to the boil over a medium–high heat, stirring. Add the strawberries and sugar, reduce the heat to low and simmer, stirring frequently, for 5 minutes until the mixture has thickened. Add the champagne and continue to simmer for a further 3–5 minutes until the mixture has thickened. Set aside to cool.

5 To make the icing, put the butter, 450 g/1 lb of the icing sugar, champagne, orange zest and orange juice into a bowl and whisk with an electric whisk until well combined. Add more icing sugar if necessary to achieve a piping consistency. Spoon into a piping bag fitted with a star-shaped nozzle.

6 To make the orange wedge decorations, divide the marzipan in half. Add a few drops of red food colouring and a few drops of yellow food colouring to one half of the marzipan and knead until evenly incorporated. Add more red colour if needed, to achieve a dark orange colour – this will be used to make the orange rind. Add a couple of drops of yellow food colouring and a couple of drops of red food colouring to the remaining piece of marzipan, using less red than before, and knead until evenly incorporated – this will be used to make the inside of the wedges in a lighter orange colour.

7 Divide both marzipan colours into 12 pieces. Take one piece of light orange marzipan and shape into a half-round about 4 mm/ ¼ inch thick. Lightly pinch the flat side of the half-round to make a wedge shape. Flatten a piece of the dark orange marzipan and press in place around the curved edge of the light orange wedge, trimming as necessary to give the effect of a peel. Repeat with the remaining marzipan to make 12 orange wedges in total. Using the edible-ink marker, draw lines on the lighter orange part to represent the inner membranes of an orange wedge. Set aside to dry.

8 Use an apple corer to remove the centre of each cupcake. Spoon the strawberry filling into the holes. Pipe the icing on to the cupcakes, sprinkle with sugar crystals, then top each cupcake with a marzipan orange wedge.

Mimosa

INGREDIENTS
serves 1
1 passion fruit
½ measure orange curaçao
champagne, chilled
star fruit slice, to decorate

METHOD
1 Scoop out the passion fruit
flesh into a shaker and shake
with the curaçao and
cracked ice until frosted.

2 Pour into a chilled
champagne flute and
top up with champagne.

3 Dress with the star fruit slice.

Maidenly Mimosa

INGREDIENTS
serves 2
175 ml/6 fl oz orange juice
175 ml/6 fl oz sparkling white
   grape juice

METHOD
1 Chill 2 champagne flutes.

2 Divide the orange juice
between the flutes.

3 Top up with the sparkling
grape juice.

Vanilla Rose Macaroons

INGREDIENTS
makes 16
70 g/2½ oz ground almonds
115 g/4 oz icing sugar
2 large egg whites
55 g/2 oz caster sugar
½ tsp vanilla extract

filling
55 g/2 oz butter, softened
½ tsp rosewater
a few drops of pink food
    colouring
115 g/4 oz icing sugar, sifted
crystalized rose petals, to
    decorate (optional)

METHOD

1 Line two baking trays with baking paper. Put the ground almonds and icing sugar into a food processor and whizz for 15 seconds. Sift the mixture into a bowl.

2 Put the egg whites into a large bowl and whip until holding soft peaks. Gradually whisk in the caster sugar to make a firm, glossy meringue. Whisk in the vanilla extract.

3 Using a palette knife, fold the almond mixture into the meringue one third at a time. When all the dry ingredients are fully incorporated, continue to cut and fold the mixture until it forms a shiny mixture with a thick, ribbon-like consistency.

4 Pour the mixture into a piping bag fitted with a 1-cm/½-inch plain tip. Pipe 32 small rounds on to the prepared baking sheets. Tap the baking sheets firmly on to a work surface to remove air bubbles. Leave at room temperature for 30 minutes. Preheat the oven to 160°C/325°F/Gas Mark 3.

5 Bake in the preheated oven for 10–15 minutes. Leave to cool for 10 minutes. Carefully peel the macaroons off the baking paper and leave to cool completely.

6 To make the filling, whisk the butter, rosewater and pink food colouring in a bowl until pale and fluffy. Gradually whisk in the icing sugar until smooth. Use to sandwich together pairs of macaroons and decorate with petals if using.

White Chocolate & Rose Cupcakes

INGREDIENTS
makes 12

115 g/4 oz butter, softened,
   or soft margarine
100 g/3½ oz caster sugar
1 tsp rosewater
2 eggs, lightly beaten
115 g/4 oz self-raising flour
55 g/2 oz white chocolate,
   grated

icing

115 g/4 oz white chocolate,
   broken into pieces
2 tbsp milk
175 g/6 oz cream cheese
30 g/1 oz icing sugar

to decorate

a few pink rose petals
1 egg white, lightly beaten
icing sugar, for dusting

METHOD

1 Preheat the oven to 180°C/350°F/Gas Mark 4 and line a 12-hole cupcake tin with paper cases.

2 Place the butter, sugar and rosewater in a large bowl and whisk together until light and fluffy. Gradually whisk in the eggs. Sift in the flour and, using a metal spoon, fold in gently. Fold in the grated chocolate.

3 Spoon the mixture into the paper cases. Bake in the preheated oven for 15–20 minutes or until a cocktail stick inserted into the centre of a cupcake comes out clean. Transfer to a wire rack and leave to cool.

4 To make the icing, put the chocolate and milk in a heatproof bowl set over a saucepan of gently simmering water and heat until melted. Remove from the heat and stir until smooth. Let cool for 30 minutes. Put the cream cheese in a separate bowl, sift in the icing sugar and whisk together until smooth and creamy. Fold in the melted chocolate. Chill in the refrigerator for 1 hour.

5 Swirl the icing over the tops of the cupcakes. To decorate, lightly brush the rose petals with a little of the beaten egg white. Sprinkle with sugar and leave to set. Arrange the sugar-frosted petals on top of the cupcakes.

Wedding Belle

INGREDIENTS
serves 1
2 measures gin
2 measures Dubonnet liqueur
1 measure cherry brandy
1 measure orange juice
orange peel strip, to decorate

METHOD
1 Put cracked ice into a cocktail shaker. Pour the liquid ingredients over the ice. Shake vigorously until well frosted.

2 Sieve into a chilled cocktail glass and decorate with the orange peel.

White Diamond Frappé

INGREDIENTS
serves 1

¼ measure peppermint
    schnapps
¼ measure white crème de
    cacao
¼ measure anise-flavoured
    liqueur
¼ measure lemon juice

METHOD

1 Put cracked ice into a
cocktail shaker. Pour the
ingredients over the ice.
Shake vigorously until
well frosted.

2 Sieve into a chilled shot
glass and add a small
spoonful of crushed ice.

Champagne is always appropriate for a grand celebration. Whether you're celebrating a graduation, a big promotion at work or a milestone birthday, sparkling Champagne Cocktails, Mimosas or Bellinis in gorgeous champagne flutes will mark the occasion in grand fashion.

Likewise, champagne, roses, hearts and sparkly stuff are all great for setting the tone for love and romance. Champagne Cocktails or Mimosas paired with White Chocolate & Rose Cupcakes are perfectly suited to a midday bridal shower. Pair Kir Royales with Chocolate Meringue Kisses for an engagement party or anniversary celebration. Celebrate a wedding with White Diamond Frappés served with Heart Cupcakes.

Warm drinks and spicy notes set a cosy tone for the winter holidays. Eggnog served with Chilli & Cardamom Chocolate Thins or Mulled Wine paired with Cranberry & Orange Mini Pies are sure to invoke a holiday spirit. Of course, a Champagne Pick-Me-Up is the perfect foil for a New Year's Day brunch.

Heart-in-a-Cupcake

INGREDIENTS
makes 12
275 g/9¾ oz plain flour
¼ tsp salt
175 g/6 oz unsalted butter,
    softened, plus extra for
    greasing
300 g/10½ oz caster sugar
1 tbsp vanilla extract
3 large eggs
400 ml/14 fl oz milk
pink food colouring
heart-shaped sprinkles, to
    decorate

icing
3 large egg whites
150 g/5½ oz caster sugar
225 g/8 oz unsalted butter,
    softened
1 tsp vanilla extract
pink food colouring

METHOD
1 Preheat the oven to 180°C/350°F/Gas Mark 4 and grease a 23-cm/9-inch round cake tin. Draw a straight line down the middle of the base (outside) of each of 12 pink or red paper cases. Put the cases in a 12-hole cupcake tin with the lines all facing the same direction. Remember which direction the lines are facing as this will show you how to align your hidden hearts.

2 Sift together the flour and salt in a bowl. Put the butter and sugar into a separate bowl and whisk until pale and fluffy. Add the vanilla extract, then add the eggs one at a time, whisking after each addition. Add half of the flour mixture and the milk and whisk until incorporated. Add the remaining flour mixture and mix.

3 Transfer about one third of the mixture to a separate bowl and mix in several drops of pink food colouring until evenly distributed. Spread the mixture evenly in the prepared cake tin and bake in the preheated oven for 18 minutes, or until the cake is just cooked. Leave to cool in the tin for 1–2 minutes, then turn out on to a wire rack and leave to cool completely (do not turn off the oven).

4 Use a 4-cm/1½-inch heart-shaped biscuit cutter to cut out 12 hearts from the pink cake. Discard the trimmings. Spoon a generous tablespoon of the remaining cake mixture into the base of one of the paper cases and then stand a heart vertically in the middle, lining it up with the line drawn on the base of the case. Spoon more mixture around the sides of the heart until the case is about two thirds full. Repeat to fill all 12 cases. Cover the mini-muffin tin with foil to prevent the prebaked hearts drying out.

5 Bake in the preheated oven for 20 minutes until a cocktail stick inserted into the centre of a cupcake comes out clean. Leave to cool in the tin for 1–2 minutes, then transfer to a wire rack to cool completely.

6 To make the icing, put the egg whites and sugar in a heatproof bowl set over a saucepan of gently simmering water and whisk over simmering water until the sugar has completely dissolved. Remove from the heat and whisk the mixture for 4–5 minutes until it holds stiff peaks. Add the butter, 25 g/1 oz at a time, and continue to whisk until it holds stiff peaks. Add the vanilla extract and several drops of pink food colouring and whisk until the colour is fully incorporated. Gradually whisk in more food colouring until the desired shade is achieved. Spoon the icing into a piping bag fitted with a star-shaped nozzle.

7 Pipe the icing on to the cupcakes and decorate with the heart-shaped sprinkles. Cut in half to serve so that the hearts will show.

French Kiss

INGREDIENTS
serves 1
2 measures bourbon
1 measure apricot liqueur
2 tsp grenadine
1 tsp lemon juice

METHOD

1 Put cracked ice into a cocktail shaker.

2 Pour the liquid ingredients over the ice.

3 Shake vigorously until well frosted.

4 Sieve into a chilled cocktail glass.

Kir Royale

INGREDIENTS
serves 1

a few drops of crème de cassis,
    or to taste
1 tbsp brandy (optional)
champagne, chilled

METHOD

1 Pour the crème de cassis
and brandy if using into a
chilled champagne flute.

2 Wait a moment and
then gently pour in the
champagne.

Chocolate Meringue Kisses

INGREDIENTS
makes 40

3 egg whites
1 tsp raspberry vinegar
150 g/5½ oz caster sugar
1 tsp cornflour
2 tbsp cocoa powder, sifted
225 g/8 oz plain chocolate,
    roughly chopped

METHOD

1 Preheat the oven to 160°C/325°F/Gas Mark 3. Line 3 baking trays with non-stick baking paper.

2 Whisk the egg whites in a large, clean mixing bowl until you have stiff, moist-looking peaks. Gradually whisk in the vinegar and sugar a tablespoon at a time until thick and glossy. Using a large metal spoon, gently fold in the cornflour and cocoa powder.

3 Spoon the mixture into a piping bag fitted with a large star nozzle and pipe 40 x 2.5-cm/1-inch 'kisses' on to the prepared baking trays.

4 Put the trays in the preheated oven, then immediately turn the heat down to 120°C/250°F/Gas Mark ½. Bake for 45 minutes or until crisp on the outside. Transfer the meringues to a wire rack, still on the paper, and leave to cool for 1 hour, then peel off the paper.

5 Meanwhile, put the chocolate into a heatproof bowl set over a saucepan of gently simmering water and heat until melted.

6 Line the baking trays with more baking paper. Dip the bases of the meringue kisses in the melted chocolate and place them, chocolate side up, on the prepared baking trays. Leave to set for 1 hour. Store in an airtight container in a cool, dry place for up to 2 weeks.

Valentine Berry Love Pies

INGREDIENTS
makes 24 individual pies
a little butter, for greasing
350 g/12 oz strawberries
2 tsp cornflour
2 tbsp strawberry jam
grated rind of 2 limes
450 g/1 lb ready-made sweet
    pastry, chilled
a little plain flour, for dusting
1 egg yolk mixed with
    1 tbsp water, to glaze
caster sugar, for sprinkling

to serve
225 ml/8 fl oz double cream
grated rind of 2 limes
2 tbsp icing sugar

METHOD
1 Preheat the oven to 180°C/350°F/Gas Mark 4 and lightly grease two 12-hole mini-muffin tins.

2 Roughly chop the strawberries. Put them in a mixing bowl and stir in the cornflour, jam and lime rind.

3 Roll out half of the pastry thinly on a lightly floured surface. Using a fluted biscuit cutter, stamp out 24 rounds each 6cm/2½ inches in diameter. Press these gently into the prepared tins, re-rolling the trimmings as needed.

4 Brush the top edges of the pastry cases with a little of the egg glaze, then spoon in the filling.

5 Roll the remaining pastry out thinly on a lightly floured surface. Use a 5-cm/2-inch heart-shape cookie cutter to cut out 24 hearts. Use the hearts as lids, pressing the edges together. Brush egg glaze over the pastry and sprinkle with caster sugar.

6 Bake in the preheated oven for 15 minutes or until a golden colour. Leave to cool in the tins for 10 minutes, then loosen with a round-bladed knife and transfer to a wire rack to cool.

7 Whip the cream until it forms soft swirls, then fold in half of the lime rind and all of the icing sugar. Sprinkle with the rest of the lime rind. Serve the pies with spoonfuls of whipped cream.

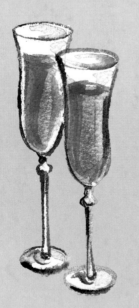

A Sloe Kiss

INGREDIENTS
serves 1
½ measure sloe gin
½ measure Southern Comfort
1 measure vodka
1 tsp amaretto
splash of Galliano liqueur
orange juice
orange peel twist, to decorate

METHOD
1 Put cracked ice into
a cocktail shaker, pour
in the sloe gin, Southern
Comfort, vodka and
amaretto and shake
until well frosted.

2 Sieve into a long chilled
glass filled with cracked ice.

3 Splash on the Galliano.

4 Top up with orange juice
and decorate with the
orange peel.

Purple Passion

INGREDIENTS
serves 1
2 measures vodka
4 measures grapefruit juice
4 measures purple grape juice

METHOD

1 Fill a chilled highball glass with cracked ice.

2 Put cracked ice into a cocktail shaker. Pour the liquid ingredients over the ice. Shake vigorously until well frosted.

3 Sieve into the glass.

For special celebrations and festive holidays, a few pretty garnishes and clever decorating techniques are all you need to make your celebration extra special. Decorate glasses by moistening the rim (we like to use a slit wedge of lemon or lime), then dip the rim in a wide bowl filled with decorating sugar or coarse salt. A wedge or twist of citrus is a lovely finishing touch for most cocktails. Garnish sweet, fruity cocktails with skewers of fruit (pineapple, kiwi fruit, grapes and berries are colourful and look fantastic), creamy drinks with peppermint sticks or savoury drinks with pickled green beans, olives, celery sticks or slices of cucumber.

For cupcakes, add heart-shaped decorations for romantic occasions, and white or shimmering metallic icing, flowers and other decorations for bridal showers and weddings. For the winter holidays let the whimsy of the season be your guide and decorate cupcakes with snowmen, tiny Santas, wrapped presents, reindeer, holly and mistletoe.

Holiday Eggnog

INGREDIENTS
makes about 1.7 litres/3 pints

6 large eggs
100 g/3½ oz plus 2 tbsp
    caster sugar
500 ml/18 fl oz single cream
500 ml/18 fl oz milk

125 ml/4 fl oz brandy
4 tbsp light rum
1 tsp vanilla extract
500 ml/18 fl oz double cream
freshly grated nutmeg

METHOD

1 Whisk the eggs with an electric whisk on medium speed until thick and a lemon colour, then gradually add the 100 g/3½ oz sugar, whisking well.

2 Put the cream and milk into a large saucepan over a medium–low heat and heat until thoroughly hot but not boiling. Gradually add the hot milk mixture to the egg mixture, stirring with a balloon whisk. Transfer the mixture back to the large saucepan and cook over a medium–low heat, stirring continuously with a balloon whisk until hot but not boiling. Remove from the heat and leave to cool. Stir in the brandy, rum and vanilla extract with a balloon whisk. Cover and refrigerate until thoroughly chilled.

3 Just before serving, whisk the double cream and the remaining 2 tablespoons of sugar in a large bowl until soft peaks form. Pour the chilled eggnog mixture into a large punch bowl. Gently fold the whipped cream into the eggnog mixture just until combined. Decorate each serving with freshly grated nutmeg.

Chilli & Cardamom Chocolate Thins

INGREDIENTS
makes 40

Chilli Chocolate Thins
225 g/8 oz plain chocolate, roughly chopped
a large pinch of hot chilli powder
edible glitter, to decorate

Cardamom White Chocolate Thins
225 g/8 oz white chocolate, roughly chopped
½ tsp cardamom seeds, crushed
25 g/1 oz pistachio nuts, finely chopped, plus extra to decorate
edible glitter, to decorate

METHOD

1 Line 4 baking trays with non-stick baking paper.

2 For the Chilli Chocolate Thins, put the plain chocolate in a heatproof bowl set over a saucepan of gently simmering water and heat until melted. Remove from the heat and stir in the chilli powder.

3 Drop teaspoonfuls of the chocolate mixture on to 2 of the prepared baking trays. Sprinkle a little of the edible glitter over the thins before the chocolate sets. Leave to set in a cool place, but not in the refrigerator, for 1–2 hours.

4 For the Cardamom White Chocolate Thins, put the white chocolate in a heatproof bowl set over a saucepan of gently simmering water and heat until melted. Remove from the heat and stir in the cardamom and pistachios.

5 Drop teaspoonfuls of the white chocolate mixture on to the remaining 2 prepared baking trays. Sprinkle the remaining chopped pistachios and a little edible glitter over the thins before the chocolate sets. Leave to set in a cool place, but not in the refrigerator, for 1–2 hours. Store in an airtight container in a cool, dry place for up to 5 days.

Mulled Wine

INGREDIENTS
serves 4

750 ml bottle red wine
2 measures sherry
8 cloves
1 cinnamon stick
½ tsp ground mixed spice
2 tbsp clear honey
1 orange, cut into wedges
1 lemon, cut into wedges

METHOD

1 Put the wine, sherry, cloves, cinnamon, mixed spice and honey into a saucepan. Warm over a low heat, stirring, until just starting to simmer, but do not allow it to boil.

2 Remove from the heat and pour through a sieve. Discard the cloves and cinnamon stick.

3 Return the pan to the heat with the orange and lemon wedges and warm gently. Pour into 4 warm heatproof glasses.

Cranberry Collins

INGREDIENTS
serves 1

2 measures vodka
¾ measure elderflower cordial
3 measures cranberry juice
soda water
lime slice and lime peel twist,
   to decorate

METHOD

1 Put cracked ice into
a cocktail shaker.

2 Pour in the vodka,
elderflower cordial and
cranberry juice and shake
until well frosted.

3 Sieve into a Collins glass
filled with cracked ice.

4 Top up with soda water
and decorate with the lime
slice and peel.

Christmas Cranberry & Orange Pies

INGREDIENTS
makes 12 individual pies

butter, for greasing
175 g/6 oz frozen cranberries
1 tbsp cornflour
3 tbsp freshly squeezed orange
   juice

2 star anise
150 g/5½ oz caster sugar, plus
   extra for sprinkling

225 g/8 oz ready-made sweet
   pastry, chilled
plain flour, for dusting
milk, to glaze

METHOD

1 Preheat the oven to 180°C/350°F/Gas Mark 4 and lightly grease a 12-hole mini-muffin tin.

2 Put the still-frozen cranberries in a medium-size saucepan along with the cornflour and orange juice. Add the star anise and cook, uncovered, over a low heat, stirring from time to time, for 5 minutes or until the cranberries have softened. Add the sugar and cook for a further 5 minutes, then leave to cool.

3 Roll out the pastry thinly on a lightly floured surface. Using a fluted biscuit cutter, stamp out 12 rounds, each 5 cm/ 2 inches in diameter. Press these gently into the prepared tin, re-rolling the trimmings as needed. Squeeze any remaining trimmings together and reserve.

4 Brush the top edges of the pastry cases with a little milk. Discard the star anise, then spoon in the filling.

5 Roll out the remaining pastry thinly on a lightly floured surface. Using a fluted pastry wheel, cut thin strips of dough. Arrange these over each pie and brush with a little milk. Sprinkle with a little sugar. Bake in the preheated oven for 20 minutes, covering with foil after 10 minutes if the tops are browning too quickly. Leave to cool in the tin for 10 minutes, then loosen with a round-bladed knife and transfer to a wire rack to cool. Serve warm or cold.

Baby Bellini

INGREDIENTS
serves 1
2 measures peach juice
1 measure lemon juice
sparkling apple juice

METHOD
1 Pour the peach juice and
lemon juice into a chilled
champagne flute and
stir well.

2 Top up with sparkling
apple juice and stir again.

Champagne Pick-Me-Up

INGREDIENTS
serves 1
2 measures brandy
1 measure orange juice
1 measure lemon juice
dash grenadine
champagne, chilled

METHOD
1 Put cracked ice into a cocktail shaker.

2 Pour in the brandy, orange juice, lemon juice and grenadine and shake vigorously until well frosted.

3 Sieve into a wine glass.

4 Top up with champagne.

Index